PAPER LANTERNS

DEEPA THOMAS DAVY

ISBN 979-888521367-7

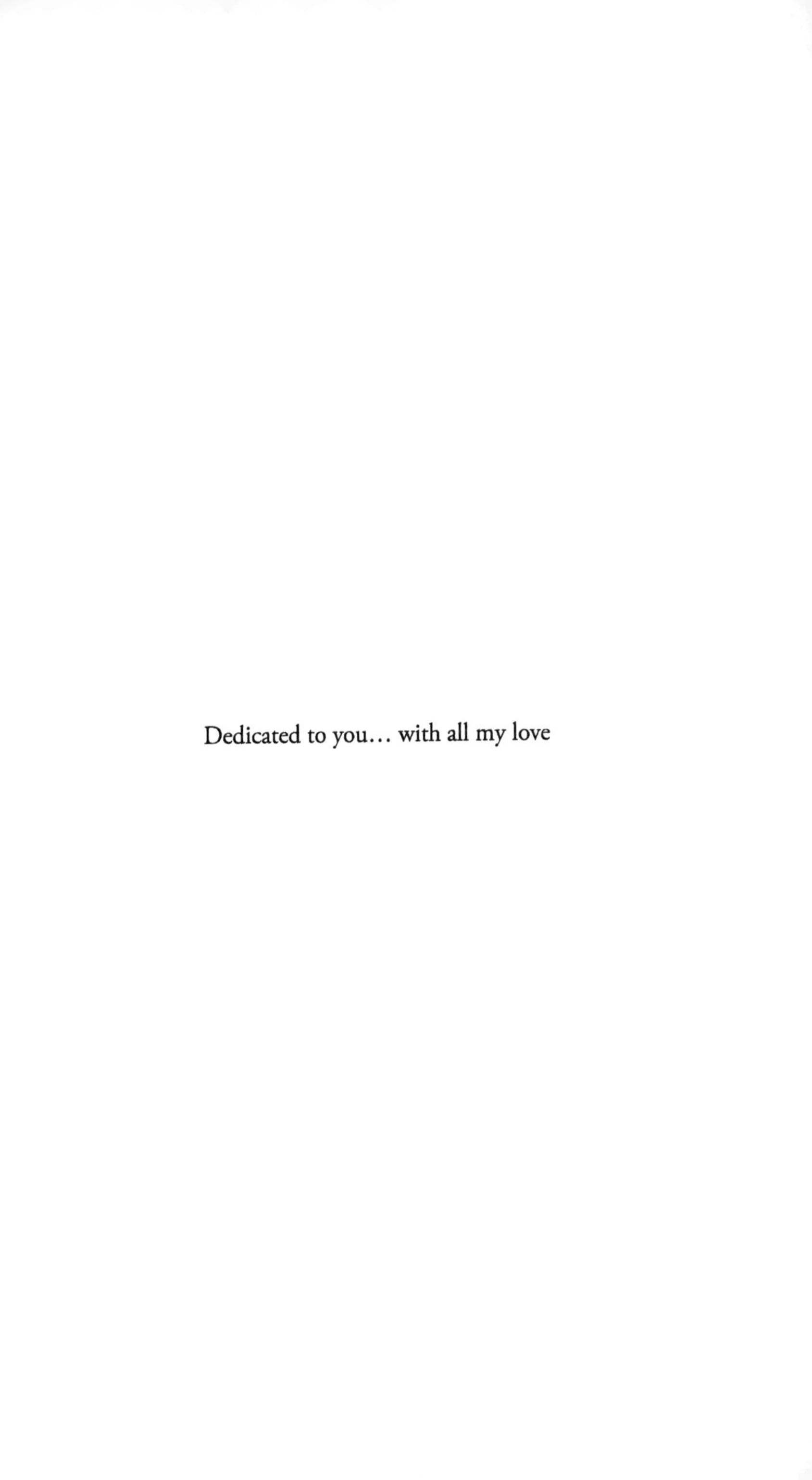

Dedicated to you… with all my love

Contents

1. Moonbeams And Waterfalls 1
2. Of Hilltops And Valleys 5
3. What Moon Is This? 8
4. Ladybugs On Leaves 10
5. The Rainbow 13
6. Reminiscence 16
7. Daisies By The Stream 20
8. The Story Of The Sun And The Moon 23
9. Rainbow Beads And Silver Bells 26
10. Fluttering Memories 27
11. The Valley 28
12. Tinged Gold 29
13. Eternal Incandescence 32
14. Grains Of Sand 34
15. A Cinderella Story 35
16. Radiance 36
17. Sunlight Dances 39
18. Pink Of Sky 41
19. Fade 43
20. Night 45
21. Dawn 46
22. Meadows Green 49
23. Pistachio Days 50
24. Tender Grace 53

Contents

25. Lipstick On The Collar 56
26. Paper Boats 59
27. The Child 60
28. Mellow Sunlight 61
29. Crushed 63
30. Aurora 65
31. Intimate Sanctity 66
32. A Lace Of Thought 68
33. Simple Joys 69
34. Eternal Sky 71
35. Jubilance 74
36. A Silver Spring 77
37. Blush Of Cloud 79
38. Cinnamon Sticks 82
39. I Know Not 83
40. Kites 84
41. Life In Watercolors 85
42. Bottle Of Stone 86
43. Transcendence 87
44. Clouds Vanilla 90
45. Slide By Slide 91
46. Imperceptible 92
47. Sometimes 93
48. Winter Breeze 95

Contents

49. Love Whispered 97
50. Tenderness 98
51. Twilight Eternity 99
52. Whispers Of Fragrance 103
53. Dreams Of Day 105
54. Strummed 107
55. Still 108
56. Misty Days 109
57. Unaware 110
58. Batik Day 111
59. Raindrop 112
60. Clouds 113
61. Twirls Of Life 114
62. Travels Of The Heart 116
63. The Jacaranda Tree 117
64. Weaving Moonlight 120
65. Sunlight Tumble 121
66. Shades Of Green 123
67. Love Me Not 124
68. The Flame 125
69. Floral Waltz 126
70. Silver Threads 127
71. You 128
72. Butterfly Stories 129

Contents

73. Cinnamon Tea 130
74. Autumned Leaves 131
75. Fluttered In 132
76. Paper Wrapped Roses 133
77. Blurred Lines 134
78. Farewells 135
79. Watercolor Feelings 136
80. Charcoaled Thoughts 137
81. The Mumble 138
82. Just Like That 139
83. When You Think Of Me 140
84. Drenched Visions 141
85. Sacred Morning 142
86. A Dream Of Nostalgia 143
87. Amber Waves 144
88. Shades And Shadows 145
89. Enflamed 146
90. Threads And Tassels 147
91. Musings From A Potter's Wheel 149
92. Constellations 151
93. Crescented Window 152
94. Smudged 153
95. Sunkist 154
96. Once 155

Contents

97. Paths Of Memory 156
98. Whispered Heart 157
99. Morning Chimes 158
100. Hushed 159
101. A Conversation 160
102. Splashed Colors 162
103. Tarnished Gold 163
104. Ethereal Show 164
105. Twilight 165
106. Why 167
107. a Wisp Of A Love 168
108. Cherished 169
109. Photographs 170
110. Paradox Of Life 171
111. Translucence 172
112. Camouflage 173
113. Snow Angels 174
114. Dandelion Dreams 175
115. Unraveling Of The Time Glass Hour 176
116. Broken Flowers 181
117. A Glance 182
118. Unkempt Tenderness 183
119. 2020 184
120. The Charm 185

Contents

121. A Gossamer Dream 186

122. The Rustle 187

123. Drops Of Light 188

124. String Of Words 189

125. Different Hearts 190

126. Just Being Me 192

127. Truthful Lies 194

128. Until You Left 195

129. Walled Ice 196

130. Softspoken Smiles 197

131. Cloudy Days 198

132. Moonlit Aurora 199

133. Angels 202

134. Spaces 206

135. Unspoken Words 207

A Note Of Gratitude 209

Deepa Thomas Davy has served many years as an educator. Her academic credentials include 3 undergraduate degrees. After several years of enriching work experience in the field of education, she was inspired to further her own studies and succeeded in earning her postgraduate degree in English Language and Literature.

Deepa discovered the joy of writing some years ago. Her poems have been published in anthologies both in India and in the United States. Paper Lanterns is her first book. She finds freedom in writing and creating her own work. She finds the experience of putting thoughts into expression, both refreshing and rejuvenating. Her main inspiration comes from nature and she is drawn to its raw energy and ethereal beauty. She believes in appreciating the simple joys of life, living in the present and cherishing each moment.

Email: sprinkledpoetry@gmail.com

Instagram handle: @sprinkledpoetry

Facebook Page: Sprinkled Poetry

Website: http://sprinkledpoetry.wordpress.com

1. Moonbeams and Waterfalls

Come away with me
To splash in the puddles
To dance in the rain
To paint in the air with fingertips vain

Come away with me to an island
Where there's only you and me

Come away with me for a while
To trace imagination with our eyes

The sky will be our ceiling
The sun our warmth

The night sky our soothing blanket
The crystal stars our lights

The tinkle of the waterfall our music
And moon beams our lamps

The roar of the river
The rustle of the leaves
And the breeze
Our tender lullabies

~ Dee

2. Of Hilltops and Valleys

I wish for a spring of cool mountain air
To lift my hair like a maenad's
To make my fingertips cool and fresh
To drizzle my face with mist

I wish for the breeze to blow through the strands
And tingle my skin
With tenderness kissed

I wish for the dew
With the wind on its back
To spritz my soul... my self... me
To wash off the tarnish of worry and strife
To renew… to refresh my life

I wish for the misty cool mountains
To gaze over hills and plains
To watch clouds unfurl
Sailing through sky
Caressing treetops
Swirling and twirling
Through flower strewn paths

I wish for the ethereal enchantment
Of firefly nights and valleys
Moonbeams
Charmed by velvet sky
Lingering
Heart on the sleeve

~ Dee

3. What Moon Is This?

What moon is this
Mellow moon
Floating in the night
Love you so
Sailing above
Gently touching our lives

Do you speak of romance
Between lovers dear
On moonlit rivers and paths
Between the trees
Beside the lake
With soft waves lapping by

Do you speak of lost loves
With tender tranquility
Do you hum a lullaby
To the brokenhearted ones

Or do you send down beams
To soothe melancholy
On moonlit tender nights
~ Dee

4. Ladybugs on Leaves

Of wildflowers
In old wine bottles
Of wine-stained lips
And laughter sweet
Of a train's rustle in the background
That steamy whistles do announce

Of orchards and open fields
Of fish in the sea
Of apples and pears
Hanging on trees
And ladybugs on leaves

Caress the grass with your feet
Grace the petals with touch serene
Gather the fallen flowers
Get lost in fragrance divine

All this I wish for you
This heavenly splendor on this good earth
To see through the eyes of a child
The wonders of the universe

~ Dee

5. The Rainbow

You knew I loved you
Long before I did
You knew I lived my days for you
Long before I said

You knew I dreamt of you
Long before I saw
Your thoughts dancing in my head

You knew the sun rose for me
When you walked into the room
My face a dim reflection when you left with someone else

You knew I cried for you
Long before I wrote
Unseen tears of tenderness

You knew you became a part of me
Without me knowing when
And now you've returned to reminisce
To recompense

~ Dee

6. Reminiscence

Let's sit down
By the river
Let's talk of yesterday

Our youth and our laughter
Our fears and our faults

Let's laugh at our failures
Let's laugh at our wins

When we become older
Our humor reminisces

We can laugh at ourselves
For the things we did
We can laugh at ourselves
For the things we didn't

Let's walk for a bit
On the petal strewn paths
While our eyes start to sparkle
With memories faded

The curve of a smile
Is always a beginning
The curve of a smile
Is always endearing

Let's stop for a bit
For a cup of tea
Let's gaze at the sky
With promises hidden
Let's dream of the hilltops
All misty ridden

A cottage
A fireplace
In the folds of green
A precious pearl hidden
In between
Beckons us inside
With warmth and peace
Of old friendships
Never forgotten
~ Dee

7. Daisies by the Stream

Daisies by the stream
Swaying in the breeze
Welcoming the newborn sun
With a wave and nod of heads
They seem to say:

Oh… you're here again
To bask in our delightful blossoms
Oh… you're here again
To borrow glory from our golden dust

The sun looks down at them carefully
Lest his bright glare should burn and burst
Their blooms balanced so delicately
On the tender stalks of green
Nods his head with a gentle smile
And softly replies:

Oh, you're right little buds so virgin white
Without your beauty to bask in every morn
Without your yellow bright to give me mine
What joy or glory should I have
From dawn to dusk as I roam
East to West every day
From sunrise to sunset

If I do not see your little bonneted heads
In snow white linen pure and true
Hiding your golden minds away
From all the dust and hue
What joy or glory should I have
From dawn to dusk as I roam
East to West every day
From sunrise to sunset

~ Dee

8. The Story of the Sun and the Moon

The careful nonchalance of the setting sun
The sensitive aloofness of the rising moon
Lovers yet they never meet
Forever mirrored in each other's hearts
A forever reflection of the other

Guardian Angels of the Earth
One by day and the other by night
Of different visions and versions
Of light and dark and of all that is right

How they kept track of time through the sky
How they traced each other through the clouds
How they lingered just before the other
Disappeared and appeared from each other

True love if it ever was
For they had each other's hearts
Pristine love it ever was
Selfless love it always shone

Laws of Nature
Laws of Attraction
Do they ever agree
Or just agree to disagree
We shall never know

A rendezvous
Of mutual perceptions
Of simple delights
On days of mathematics
Occur
And for those days and memories
They live forever more
The golden sun and the silver moon
Their eternal story written in the sky

~ Dee

9. Rainbow Beads and Silver Bells

Somethings you lose along the way
Without realizing they are lost
Like a gypsy trundling along
Rainbow beads and silver bells
Carelessly sprinkled everywhere
When the silence makes her pause and wonder
About the missing silver clatter
It's too late, it's too late
To wander back
It's too late
To pick up those silver bells and rainbow beads
It's too late
For they have disappeared without a trace

~ Dee

10. Fluttering Memories

How easily memories flutter down
From a tree left unshaken for so long

Red and green
Orange of hue
Yellow pink and blue

Black and grey
And white so true
Tender memories of you

Soft and gentle they float down
To fill my lap with love so true

Delicate they balance and pirouette
To fill my heart with cheer still yet
Though I never told you
Know my love for you is true

~ Dee

11. The Valley

Copper Bells
Temple bells
High up in the mountains
Echoing through the hilltops
Floating through the clouds

Verdant meadows
Dew covered fields
Delicate daisies swaying in the breeze
Butterflies wafting from bloom to bloom
Coloring the green grass a rainbow hue

Waterfall splashes to a cadence of its own
A scene of beauty for tired eyes
A soothing sound of joyful peace

A breeze passes through with mist on its wings
A movement of delight to the passersby
A moment to refresh their weary minds
Immersed in the joy that it brings

~ Dee

12. Tinged Gold

The sun traversed the bright blue sky
Tinged the earth with a gold so bright
Gleaming and glinting with strength and might
Glamorous shenanigans up too high

The demure clouds gaze
Await with patience and a gentle sigh
For a cool breeze and cooler days
To refresh the earth and sky

The sun bids adieu
With gentle peach
Baby pink tinges
Dainty rose blush
Coral edges to the day gone by

The clouds surround to bid good night
And he softly whispers
His love and delight
For this blessed day~ so golden bright
~ Dee

13. Eternal Incandescence

Of jasmine drops
And amethyst wings
In a fairy field of lush
I can gaze at you
I can gaze at you
Forever

The morning blush from the rising sun
The evening flush
Of newborn spring
The dew still quivering
On the morning brow
The wildflowers sway in the morning breeze
The fresh new scene of the golden day
I can gaze at you
I can gaze at you
Forever

The dusk has come and the setting sun
The velvet sky
The stars each one
Whisper and twinkle light and high
The gentle moon and moonlit nights
I can gaze at you
I can gaze at you
Forever
Eternal Incandescence
~ Dee

14. Grains of Sand

Like grains of sand, each of us
So small in this great world

It's by chance and charm we meet
And our paths crossed somewhere once

Sometimes we meet again
And sometimes we do not

But it was always meant to be
That we met once before

Paths meant to cross will always cross
People meant to meet will always meet
An imprint on the heart we will always keep
Even if we meet no more

~ Dee

15. A Cinderella Story

The music's over
The dance is done

Standing alone on the dance floor
My love has walked away
And all is said and done

And I'm standing there
In my silk dress
Wishing I could run

But then
The dress will come undone
The glass slippers will break
The magic will crack
The crystal carriage
Into a pumpkin shell become

~ Dee

16. Radiance

Immerse yourself
In the radiance of light

Tiptoe by
the shore

Let the waves caress your feet
And your laughter ring out evermore

The golden grains
The blue so cool
The warmth of sun
In your soul

Embrace the warmth
Feel the spray
Shake the water away

Traipse your way
Through the sand
Tapping sounds of shells in hand
~ Dee

17. Sunlight Dances

A wistful wish
For the rain
For the clouds to gather
For the breeze to blow
For pitter patter
On the streets below

Umbrellas to open
Freshness to reign
Cool breezy weather
To blow open the drapes

Oh the temptation
To play in the rain
Even the mighty sun can't resist
The temptation to play

The sunlight dances in the rain
Each drop turns into myriad rays
Dewdrops awash with golden light
Carried away by the radiant sun
The glorious beauty of the rainbow awakes

- Dee

18. Pink of Sky

Fairy lights dotted the hills
Like firefly lamps at night

Constellations glowed
In the valley carved below
Twinkled in our eyes

Our words were mist
Blown puff by puff
Like cigarettes in our hands

The crickets chirped
The jasmines bloomed
Our footsteps trudged the night

Floral scents of dew
Settled on our face
Dew drops skimmed our hair

As we sat
Quiet and still
For the pink of sky

As we waited
Gently still
For the edge of dawn
~ Dee

19. Fade

Before I fade from your eyes
Remember that I loved you

Before I fade from your mind
Remember that I loved you

Before I fade from your heart
Remember that I loved you

In the only way I knew how to
In the only way I still do

~ Dee

20. Night

It's a midnight twinkle
In the deep velvet sky

The hum of the trees
The lull of the breeze
Makes a perfect lullaby

The crystal stars do shine
The complacent moon
smiles soft

While we rest our minds
With our restless
perfectly perfect
painted tainted dreams
of time

~ Dee

21. Dawn

There is something sacred about the dawn
As the world just begins to rouse itself from deep slumber
Trying to remember the dreams dreamt about

There is something sacred about the dawn
The magic of tousled strands of moonlight
And the fairylight stars in the morning

There is something sacred about the dawn
When the noise of the day hasn't spoken yet
When the cool morning breeze
Makes its presence known
With a tenderness every now and then

There is something sacred about the dawn
When the gift of a new day gently unfurls
Something fresh
Something beautiful
Unfolds in our minds
As we watch the hushed mornings
Blossom into day
~ Dee

22. Meadows Green

Swirling thoughts of yet unseen dreams
Fragments and patches of broken wishes
Among the fields of yellow and green

The heavens break open for a soft sun ray
To glimmer and glance onto the innocence below
Of pure brooks and rivers, the forest and the trees
Of meadows green and mountain peaks

~ Dee

23. Pistachio Days

You are the sun
You are the moon
You are the rain caressing me

You are the stars on a moonless night
The clouds in the clear blue sky
The wildflowers swaying in the breeze
The smell of fresh cut grass in the afternoon

The laughter as we jumped through sprinklers
Wet hair wet faces
Brown tanned skin
As we clapped and laughed with glee
Squelchy squishy grass between our feet
Barefoot and wanton as we pleased
Not bothered by time or what the future holds

You are the joy that cannot be described
You are the feeling no words can express
You are the intrinsic moments lost in time
You are my childhood… my pistachio days

~ Dee

24. Tender Grace

I wish you peace
As soft as morning dew
To settle on your wounded heart
To lift the veils from those sad eyes
To help you through across the days

I wish you comfort
As gentle… as feather light
To settle on your wounded soul
To see you through these hard times
To help you through across the nights

Words like wisps of lace
Floating by
Above
Below
Through
Without knowing how to carry
Tender grace
To soothe away the wrinkled worries of Time

I wish for you soft moments
Of healing peace
Feather soft petals of quietness
Soothing brush of voices near
To comfort and ease your very soul
~ Dee

25. Lipstick on the Collar

Lipstick on the Collar
And what does it say

Floral perfume
Lingering
And it's not yours
You say

Smoky eyes and smoky rooms
Dimmed lights
And cheap perfume

Lipstick on the collar
And what does it say

Is it time for you
To stay or walk away

Lipstick on the collar
The stain of a silly story

Lipstick on the collar
The end or the beginning
~ Dee

26. Paper Boats

A brush stroke of sun
A whisper of air
A brook of running water
Shimmering in the flare

Sunbeams comb through
Reflecting and gleaming

Paper boats floating by
Carrying
Innocent laughter
Childish grins
Charms of silver
Charms of gold
In this precious life we hold

~ Dee

27. The Child

The sun rose
Weaving light into shadows
A hum of hope and joy
Into the braided fields of love

And he stood
With his soft gentle eyes
And his bruised broken heart
Crossed hands and a stubborn smile

What was I to say
What was I to do
Except take him in my heart
Hug him with my soul
And love him evermore

~ Dee

28. Mellow Sunlight

New day new hopes and promises
Of all things bright and beautiful
Be blessed

New hopes new dreams arrive on beams of morning ray
Quiet still quiet still
Enjoy the peace of the day

Rest your mind
Refresh your soul
Replenish your spirit and set it free
For nothing is as complicated as first it seems to be

Golden silence be yours today
To spend in thoughtful reverie
Silver streams of joy be there
To glow and shine throughout your way

Mellow sunlight in the air
Prayers for joy and peace abound
Health and wealth and wisdom too
As our day begins with golden light
Of all things bright and beautiful
Be blessed

~ Dee

29. Crushed

Crushed rain
Crushed ice
Lipstick-stained skin
Holding me
Pressed

Lips crushed
Red stained
Drenched cold

Crushed lips
Crushed me
Crushed ice on skin
~ Dee

30. Aurora

The calmness of the meadow
The stillness of the pond

Serene moonlight
Warm sunlight
No boundaries
No walls

Aurora
The fresh dawn
As it breaks unvarnished
Unfiltered

The rustic charm of the countryside
Mango trees
Wildflowers
Glowing in morning dew

~ Dee

31. Intimate Sanctity

Somethings are not created
To be named into words
For it is yours
To be thought of
For it is yours
In that freedom of thought
Undefined
That sparkle
Twinkling in the air

Somethings cannot be described
The words that define
Have not been created yet
To express
The depth
The light
The joy

Somethings by naming them
Intimate sanctity is removed
With words and labels
The delicate grace
Of what was
Of what is
Of kindness
Of love

~ Dee

32. A Lace of Thought

A whispered touch
A lace of thought
Feathered dreams
Of tender grace

Memories playfully tousled
Tossed with laughter and cheer
Braided love in between
Glimpses here and there seen

Moments
Softly gathered
Loosely knotted
A ribbon of joy
Holding all together

~ Dee

33. Simple Joys

Blowing bubbles or flying a kite
Smelling a flower or feeling the rain

Watching the sunset or birds taking flight
The painted sky of glorious shades

The moon and her sparkly stars
The night glow in the velvety sky

Innocent moments of simple joy
Innocent moments of simple delight
~ Dee

34. Eternal Sky

Mankind looks up at the sky
For answers for reasons
In fascination in wonderment
With admiration with curiosity

To find location to find bearing
Seeking solace seeking balance

In times of love and joy
In times of sadness and desperation
In times of hope and hopelessness.

In appreciation of nature and beauty
To soothe the eyes and clear the mind.

And the sky is always there eternal
Giving us the permanence that we seek

What we find is up to us
For often it is what we seek that we find
~ Dee

35. Jubilance

The jubilance of a waterfall
As it dances in the wind
Rejoicing in life
And all the gifts it brings

It views the hills and valleys
And all the glory which surrounds
Then welcomes with wild abandon
As it rushes to the ground

Joyfully caresses
In childlike wonder
Admiration follows
As it flows through our world
Artery of abundant life

You can hear the joy and laughter
In the rivers that you see
In the streams and the brooks
As it flows down to the sea

The beauty of a waterfall
Untamed and wild
Dwells in our hearts
Vibrant and alive

A white sail of spray
Raised in joy
Innocent mirth
Misty laughter
Echoing
From up on top high
- Dee

36. A Silver Spring

A silver spring
A gentle brook
A small and cozy little nook
For me to sit
In silence peace
And contemplate the nature green

A shady tree
Lends its lace
Shields me from the ray of sun
A little peace
A little smile
A little shade
To rest a while
~ Dee

37. Blush of Cloud

Winter skies
Blushing clouds
Burnished canvas
Glory seen

Cool crisp air
To refresh the soul
Uplifts the spirit
All the while

Charming windchimes
Ringing on the breeze

The rain
The sweet cool rain
Drops of joy from heaven above
Pitter patter everywhere

The wind
Carrying dew on its wings
Cool mist on skin
Tousling hair as it whispers
Caressing teasing
Drawing patterns
In air
~ Dee

38. Cinnamon Sticks

Cinnamon sticks
Broken in a pile
Something like our broken smiles

The one who has known a broken you
A broken you and a broken me

Mended hearts
Sit awhile

Mended smiles
Be still awhile

~ Dee

39. I Know Not

Do not break my heart
For I know not what to do

Do not break my heart
For I know not where to go

Do not break my heart
For I know not how to cry

Do not break my heart
For I know not when to sigh

Do not break my heart
For I know not why you do

~ Dee

40. Kites

Unrestrained
Unattached
Like a kite flown free

Random words in easy exchange
Words flow free

Like breeze
Through elephant grass
Dances smoothly

Like a river
Over pebbles
Rounded softly

Unfettered
Unfiltered
Conversations
Among friends

~ Dee

41. Life in Watercolors

Rain and life in watercolors
Paintbrush dipped in shades
Of hue

Who you are and where you are
No matter
My soul sings so true

Everything brighter and clearer
Clarity and shine
All the time

Rain and life in watercolors
Translucence among the gray

Rain and life in watercolors
Puddles along the way

Rain and life in watercolors
Make it worthwhile anyway

~ Dee

42. Bottle of Stone

Open your hands
What do you see

Evergreens
Or dried up weeds

Is the charm there
Or is it all gone

Like the dregs at the bottom
Of the bottle of stone

~ Dee

43. Transcendence

As you wander up and down
Miss the warmth and the glow
I don't know where you go

I stare up at the moon
She doesn't meet my eyes
She knows the truth
Reflected on her face
But she won't pay the price
She doesn't want to lie

So I wait for the dawn
And I see you saunter by
The horizon blush
A telltale sign

And no you won't speak
But you glow and glimmer
Settling into your place
Allotted by the sky

The warmth that you give
Is enough for me to live
The light that you give
Abundantly alive
Enough for me to bloom

Effortless love radiances forth
Showering me in golden transcendence pure
Evoking invoking
My soul within
~ Dee

44. Clouds Vanilla

Dappled sunshine on a gentle face
Reflected skies in your liquid eyes

Tendrils wisping about your face
Clouds vanilla floating by

A smile that starts from the eyes
Catches in the throat
A sigh

~ Dee

45. Slide by Slide

I wish for a sweet train ride
With cool mountain air
Playing with my hair
The breeze kissing away all my cares

Lush scenes of green and waterfalls
Passing by... slide by slide

Such is life itself
Passing by... slide by slide

~ Dee

46. Imperceptible

She will move
Imperceptible at first
Each time you are unfair
She will move away from you

She still smiles
Because she's nice
Not because of anything you do

She will leave
To find herself
Each time you are unfair
She will move away from you
Imperceptible at first

~ Dee

47. Sometimes

There's closeness and there's apart
There's nothing and then the heart
There's the missing and the tears
When no one else is near

No matter how far
You are there in my heart
No matter how long
You will always be near

For once we felt as one
For once we thought as one
Time cannot wash away
What we felt there and then

Hold me soft
Wipe my tears
Put your hand on me
And steer me clear

Sometimes there are no words
Sometimes there is nothing
Sometimes just silence is enough
For understanding

Sometimes there are words
Sometimes there are whispers
Sometimes they flow between souls
To knit hearts together

~ Dee

48. Winter Breeze

Soft sun rays off a gossamer web
A dew drop hangs between
Radiating rainbow shades
In a crystalline sheen
Beauty in sheerness is seen

Open your hands
Open your mind
Unclench those fingers of thine
Let those who leave... leave
Let those who stay.... stay
The force of expectation has no role to play
in this play of mine

Obligations... just a charade
To mimic and mime
If there's no sincerity beneath anytime

Sometimes silence is truest and most genuine than any words heard
Sometimes listening is more important than any consolation said
Sometimes the winter breeze is more consoling than any word read

~ Dee

49. Love Whispered

Love whispered as quiet as quiet can be
Like a gentle sigh on a stirred breeze
Loosely weaving comfort into words
Misting softness into laughter

In my quietest moments of windswept thoughts
An inkling of understanding gently gleams
And I realize that it was love after all
Unknown to me
Which lay forlorn forgotten

~ Dee

50. Tenderness

Tenderness wafted through
Swirling around my lonely thoughts
Honey kissed sunshine filtered in
And I blessed the words that brought them in

~ Dee

51. Twilight Eternity

Indulgent shyness of the graceful moon
In a salt and peppered sky
Dash of sunshine in the East
Ushered silence
A golden dawn nearby

Eternal partners
In twilight cycle
Of sunsets and moonlight
Lovers but they never meet
Under the sky's watchful eye

Twined yet through space
Correlation cannot be denied
For he is reflected in her eyes
And in her glow he delights

Cupid's arrow
Never did spare nor separate
Differentiate it did not
From what could or could not be
An arrow in a little boy's hand
Holds careless wisdom randomly

Presently
We witness
Every day and every night
Cupid's mischief in the heavens
Of color shaded sky

Auroras of glory
Crescendo sunsets
When he shows off for her
Painting the sky
Myriad shades of brilliance

In a magnificent reply
She lingers past the glitter of night
Out from the comfort of dark velvet sky
Waiting for a glimpse of him in crystal light
Her ethereal beauty in the morn
Gracing the dawn
Patiently seeking the first sunbeam
Giving a glance of love before she leaves

The Sun and the Moon
Loyalty true
Eternal love it always was
Displayed on the canvas of the sky
For the whole universe to watch and sigh
~ Dee

52. Whispers of Fragrance

You were with me in the day
You were with me at night
You were with me in the morning twilight

You were with me on nights
That I found no sleep
You were with me at times
When I could not speak

What can I say
What can I sigh
To the jasmine tree
Outside

Quiet as gracious grace
Whispers of fragrance
Floating by
~ Dee

53. Dreams of Day

Sleep on a moonbeam
Wake on a sun ray
Dream on a moonlit sigh

Smile
And a half smile
On a daydream
Outside

Daffodils and dandelions
Oh so dainty on the eyes
As pillow clouds go floating by

The smell of grass
The sun on face
The birds go swinging by
Sweet melodies singing on a breeze
Wisps of color in the sky
~ Dee

54. Strummed

Was it love's soft breath
On the fingertips of my soul
That strummed the strings
Of this weary heart so long ago

~ Dee

55. Still

Was it love
I do not know

All that I know is
On some days
I miss you still

With all the tenderness of my heart
I hold you still

~ Dee

56. Misty Days

Misty roads and misty trees
Everything clothed in mist and cloud
Life's edges so softly blurred
Something we can smile about
Misty place you have my heart
Misty space you have my love
Bathed my soul in gentle ways
Graced my mind in tender waves

~ Dee

57. Unaware

And sometimes we do not know what we need
And sometimes we do not know that we love
Yet you recognized it in me
When I myself was unaware

~ Dee

58. Batik Day

Lipstick-stained glasses
Doodles on napkins
Wine-stained white tablecloth
Words carelessly played
Haze caressing spaces

In between
Carvings of day
Settle on the horizon
Shreds of night
Etched in sky
A batik day of light and shadow

~ Dee

59. Raindrop

The life of a raindrop
Fall from the heavens
Fall onto the ground
Fall on the leaves
And the treetops around

Shatter into a million
Myriad of colors
Dazzle and dance
Nourish and help

Then disappear and appear
In the rainbow above

~ Dee

60. Clouds

The sky is always blue as blue
So calm and serene above it all
Reflections are a part of life
And sometimes the robes change hue

The clouds are floaty
Playing truant and true
Sometimes grey and sometimes white
Sometimes pink and orange bright
Dulcet shades, delicate pink and rose
Brilliant degrees of bright and gold
Sometimes violet sometimes blue
Sometimes like me and sometimes like you

Clouds of mischief floating around
Forming fancy shapes with glee
Free to create and free to bless
This Earth from heaven above and us

~ Dee

61. Twirls of Life

The night air carries fragrance
The crispness cools my skin
Orion twinkles in the distance
Taunting me for my sins

Constellations shine and glimmer
Teasing me to smile and shimmer
Love beckons in the velvet sky
Too far to be seen, a substantial lie

Music on repeat...round and round
The smoke keeps swirling all around
Cans of coke and friends abound
Twirling sweetness all around
Weaving laughter into lives

The ones we miss are never here
To share our laughter or our lies
Love and laughter ours forever
Love and laughter temporal as ever

A fairy world with golden dust
A world where words hold no trust
Promises and words soon forgotten
To fit the needs of the present tense
The broken hearts soon begotten
From friends and foes with no sense

~ Dee

62. Travels of the Heart

Where have you left your heart behind this time
In one of those silver stars so high
In a tender blossom bloom on a hilltop far away
In a translucent crystal snowflake so white
In a cream-colored shell with the ocean waves on the sand
Or fitting smugly in someone else's hand

~ Dee

63. The Jacaranda Tree

The delicate purple petalled out
In the meadow green
An ocean of rainbow blooms
Swaying in the breeze

Golden sunshine fell through leaves
Dappled fields below
Winds of light on the grass
Braided into trees

Thoughts released into that sky blue air
Freed my mind
From restrictions placed there

The wind caressed my face
Tousled my hair
Careless mischief in its wayward path

Hummed wind washed over me
Eyes traced rustled trees
The brook lingered over a melody
Under the jacaranda tree where
Sprinkled butterflies kept me company
~ Dee

64. Weaving Moonlight

Weaving moonlight
Into night
Brushed canvas of the stars
Silhouettes and shadows
Poured out in shade
Splashed in purple strokes

Gingerly she steps out with a sigh
Nestled between the clouds
Moonbeams comb through
Meadows and sky
Seeking shades of gold
Flickering burnt
On the chariot of the sun

An Eastern glimpse
Burnished tinged
In the paper lanterned sky
A transcendent canvas of glory pink
On which aurora has dawned

~ Dee

65. Sunlight Tumble

The sunlight tumbles over me
In tangled confusion
Caressing my soul
A liquid gold waterfall
On my hair and my nose

The warmth absorbed
Through tingling skin
A joyous rejuvenation
Of welcoming day

The moonlight takes more care
Lingering in air
Silvery beams
Brushing deep velvet night
Gazing at me curiously
In ethereal light

With uplifted face
I examine the grace
Of ebony sky
A canvas of creations
Painted above in silvery light

~ Dee

66. Shades of Green

Come with me and let us walk
Along the flower strewn paths
Let us walk under shades of green
Where the cool breeze still lingers
among branches
Where leaves still hang
with dew soft drops after rain
Where wildflowers are our companions on either side
And we shall talk of this and that
And sometimes not at all
And still feel happy that our footsteps match
Treading soft silence in tranquil calm
~ Dee

67. Love Me Not

Love me but do not fall in love with me
For I am not worth it
Love me but do not fall in love with me
For I am trouble
Love me but do not fall in love with me
For I am as unpredictable as the weather.

~ Dee

68. The Flame

So she danced closer to the flame
Glowing liquid gold
Beckoned more and more

She swayed and swooned till she could no dance no more
When sense prevailed and addiction failed

A wounded heart pondered
How this could be

Crestfallen that it was passion which burnt her so
Singed wings carried her away cold
And passion charmed her never more

~ Dee

69. Floral Waltz

Jasmine tantalizingly shakes her head
Perfumed curls jostle for space

Frangipani reminisces
Of sultry days and sultry nights

Gardenia wafts in
Casually exotic or shy
It's hard to tell
She hasn't made up her mind

Floral scented nightfall air
Waltzes
In the spaces in between
Stilted conversations
Erratic silence
Cold passion
Chilled smiles on ice

~ Dee

70. Silver Threads

The breeze will trace your face
With dew winged grace
In the glow of morning
Tendrils of spring in your hair
A sigh on the breath of the early morn
A thread of silver thought
A golden yarn of dreams
Balled up at the feet of silken sheets
~ Dee

71. You

Love you for the words you say
Love you for the words you don't

Love you for being here
Love you for being there

Near or far
It's all the same

You make me laugh
You make me smile
You make me delight
In you

~ Dee

72. Butterfly Stories

Listen to the stories the butterflies say
Of patience
Of struggle
Of beauty
Of flight
Of impossible dreams they saw at night.
Of heaven
In a world of nectar and blossoms
- Dee

73. Cinnamon Tea

Patterned sidewalks
Dappled trees
Shadowed leaves
And latticed blooms
Edgewise sunshine
In mellow rooms
Wisps of steam
From sweet cinnamon tea
~ Dee

74. Autumned Leaves

Rippled lakes and autumned leaves
Skimming breeze and paddled oars
Warmth of love and cheer of laughter
Seasoned boats and pink parasols
Floating by on a summer's breath
~ Dee

75. Fluttered In

Fell in love
When it was not meant to be
All the parts
Of that fragile heart
So tenderly brave
Without warning
Fluttered into my soul
Tempting me
~ Dee

76. Paper Wrapped Roses

Because I loved you
And your paper wrapped roses
You sprinkled my days with laughter
You rained my days with joy
~ Dee

77. Blurred Lines

She was his for just a while
His hold so tender
She didn't feel
The way he cramped her
And blurred the lines
~ Dee

78. Farewells

It is with the last farewell
We remember the first hello
It is when people leave
We remember how first we met
~ Dee

79. Watercolor Feelings

What is this I feel
Watercolor feelings
On pink tinged paper
Edges scorched orange
Passioned and burnt
~ Dee

80. Charcoaled Thoughts

Charcoaled on canvas
A pensive thought
Imagination festive behind the scenes
Calm pastels
Vivid vibrants
Waiting impatiently
To fill up the shades
Left by reverie
- Dee

81. The Mumble

I mumbled incoherently
And Love listened ever so carefully
At the end
Belly-laughed with eyes that twinkled
Love left me
All a wrinkled
~ Dee

82. Just Like That

I love because I do
Just like that
I smile because of you
Just like that
You make me happy, yes you do
Just like that
But now I have to go, yes I do
Just like that
~ Dee

83. When You Think of Me

When you think of me
Think of me with kindness
For I was never as perfect
As you wished me to be
And as I never claimed to be
~ Dee

84. Drenched Visions

Drenched visions come to mind
The sound of pitter patter
On the streets
On the rooftops
On the umbrellas bobbing by

The coolness of the breeze
Carrying mist and dew
Gently dancing around
Swishing past
This parched earth sighs for it
As the hot winds blow

~ Dee

85. Sacred Morning

Sacred morning
Soft dawn breaking
Wind chimes in whispered breeze
Cool and mild on skin

Clarity tingles in the air
Breath a tinge of mist

People waking from warmth of slumber
Wondering what this glorious day brings
Unexpected promises and simple joys
Sprinkled through fresh of day

Dew on grass
Lifting mist on green
The peace of silence
Of purity serene

~ Dee

86. A Dream of Nostalgia

A sudden longing
For the lingering fragrance of night flowers
Wafting in on cool dusky air
Against a backdrop of cricket symphony

The toot of a cautious car
The rumble of a street cart
Selling the toasty warmth of peanuts
Dressed in paper cones
The comfort of conversation murmur
The exuberance of joyous laughter
As we laugh at each other and ourselves

The smell of grass and earth after rain
Lingering in the corridors of our memory

~ Dee

87. Amber waves

Yellow roses placed
In pristine purity of space

Silent prayers spoken
In golden solitude

Souls speak in gentleness
In solid peace surrounds

Wisps of fragrance twirl softly
Amber waves of sound

Love washes over me
Unconditionally

~ Dee

88. Shades and Shadows

When the world is in such a hurry
And the people are in such a rush
It's nice to slow the pace
To linger behind the race

Shy away from crowds
Get lost in shades and shadows
Walk barefoot on the grass

Alone yet not lonely
A calm of delight

- Dee

89. Enflamed

Take my breath away
With your beauty

Redeem me speechless
With your grace

The warmth of your love showers over me
Sunbeams on my upturned face

Just with a stroke of your finger
Just with a brush of your hand

Colors the whole sky with your essence
Passion enflamed exquisiteness

~ Dee

90. Threads and Tassels

Go then down to the meadows
To harvest blooms abundant
In a field grown thick with petals
Rainbow of flowers on earth

Buds and blossoms arrayed in glory
In a basket tenderly gathered
To be perfectly groomed

A whispered touch
A lace of thought
A glimpse of ribbon
Peeking through
Fragile delicate fern fronds
Lend grace to blossoms bloomed

Silver threads and tassels
Embellishments embolden
A symphony of elegance in varied shades
An elated bouquet transformed
With peppered eloquence graces
A gathered beauty to behold

The art of happiness generously sought
The art of happiness generously brought
Portrayed by a bouquet of memories and blossoms
Holding the fragrance of joy within

~ Dee

91. Musings from a Potter's Wheel

Mold me with your fingers
Mold me with your mind
Take the clay and form me
Creation on your side

A pot to be cooked in
Or hold water to quench thirst
A vase perhaps
to hold the blooms
A sculpture to be admired
A statue for worship
To give people hope
To give people strength
And some way to cope

Mold me with your fingers
Mold me with your mind
Work with love
Work with care
Be kind to me and do not tear
I am soft and pliant be

Once I am formed and take my shape
In the fire I will be baked
Handle with love
Handle with care
Then I am not soft
Not anymore
But fragile as fragile can be
And my heart will break
If I fall

Handle me soft
Handle me gentle
Handle with love
Handle with care

~ Dee

92. Constellations

Moonbeams descend midst fairy lights
Sprinkling silver thoughts
On upturned faces
As we wonder in starlight
The night skied constellations
Holding still in
Profound peace

~ Dee

93. Crescented Window

Mellowed warmth pouring out
Through crescented window above
Comfort of cuddled wool and yarn
Lanterned windowed radiance
Falls out into evening sky

~ Dee

94. Smudged

Candlelight
Danced on skin
Smudged kohl
Smudged lips
A matte painting
On canvas

- Dee

95. Sunkist

Perfumed tenderness
Warmth of skin
In the dusky hollows
Blurred into
Sun kissed sheets

~ Dee

96. Once

Once upon a time
I loved you
I still do
But you're not my poison anymore

~ Dee

97. Paths of Memory

Every little word of love
Written in heartbreak
Turns into a love poem
Tracing paths of memory
~ Dee

98. Whispered Heart

Now what I ask to my whispered heart
What have you got to say for yourself
As usual... there's no reply
She has better things to do
Then listen to a rational mind
And has wandered off as usual

~ Dee

99. Morning Chimes

The whispered trace
Through latticed sunshine
The golden tinged curtained lace
Charmed shaded pools
Of quiet space
Before the fluttered tendrils of day
Intrudes
Morning is chimed
~ Dee

100. Hushed

When the world in hushed silence
Awaits the dawn

Words seem whimsical and frivolous
In this quietness of grace

The shy day emerges before us
Blushing rippling pink
To make of her what we will

Welcome her with love
Welcome her with gratitude
This precious gift of day we have been given

The treasure of time
Priceless immeasurable

~ Dee

101. A Conversation

A conversation
About long forgotten mango trees
And shady paths
Strewn with fallen frangipani
Still fragrant
In cream and pink
~ Dee

102. Splashed Colors

The splashed colors of the clouds
The splotches of pink and grey
The golden ochre of transcendent sunsets
Have brought us to this day
The luminescence of the rising moon
And the presence of it in the morning blue
All orchestrated into gifting us
This glorious new day

~ Dee

103. Tarnished Gold

Golden globe of tarnished gold
Flaming fire it holds so still
For us to stare in awe
And drink in the majesty of it all

~ Dee

104. Ethereal Show

The awakening glory of the rising sun
The glow of satisfaction reflected in the skies above
As he starts his travels of the day
Culmination of beauty in ethereal show
Where he colors his desires on the clouds with love
On a day well spent before resting his head
The serenity of the moon to soothe away
In hushed whispers of comfort the cares of the day
The sprinkles of stars to gently show
The moments of joy which happened today
The blanket of dark velvet
To comfort and gently rock
On a soft lullaby.

~ Dee

105. Twilight

Pristine
Snowflakes
On the mountain top
Like little angels on earth

Reflected sunlight
On the white
A sight of glory
To behold

A pink blush
An orange flush
Up on that mount of mist

Morning twilight
Evening twilight
Time
Between
Dawn and Dusk

A luscious mauve
A red berry purple
Aurora and the rising sun
~ Dee

106. Why

Why do you ask
If I love you
You know it more
Than I do

~ Dee

107. A Wisp of a Love

Shimmering drops
Sailing leaf to leaf
Tenderly let go by trees
Mid air a drop of soft rain
Held but for a moment
Like a kiss in a dream
A wisp of a love
~ Dee

108. Cherished

Each and every time I see you
I whisper to myself I love you
It will only be whispered

Each and every time I see you
I remember the tenderness
It will only be remembered

Each and every time I see you
I think of the comfort
It will only be thought of

Each and every time I see you
I know you have touched my heart
As only you knew how to
It will be quietly cherished

- Dee

109. Photographs

In old albums
Memories
To have and to hold

Frozen time fragments
Frozen in space
In forgotten albums
All ragged and torn

Outline with fingers
Shadows of memories
Old photographs
Faded mellow gold

~ Dee

110. Paradox of Life

A stranger can become a friend
A friend can become a stranger
A stranger can become a friend once more
In a heartbeat
Everyone is just a smile away

The years don't stand in between
It's just like it was before
It happens
It happens
With old friends
Who don't care
Why you never called

~ Dee

111. Translucence

Translucence softly glows
Once loved
Can we unlove

Common Sense with deft fingers
Weaves herself here and there

She has failed ere before
But yet again she tries

But Love with gentle strength
Is unaware of Common Sense

~ Dee

112. Camouflage

The wind ruffles
The trees rustle
And there is freedom in that
When thoughts leave your floating mind
Carried away on a breeze
Rain
A perfect camouflage
For those soft tears you weep

- Dee

113. Snow Angels

The warmth of sun
Caresses skin
In the winter chill
The sunshine
Unfurls the soul from deep within

Crystals glimmer on treetops serene
Snow angels fallen
Look up at the shimmer
Glistening fairy dust
Falling in between

~ Dee

114. Dandelion Dreams

To fall asleep on butterfly wings
And to dream of beautiful things
A lily
A rose
A jasmine fine
Dandelion dreams
In a field of green
Dew dropped grass
In meadow divine
~ Dee

115. Unraveling of the Time Glass Hour

May gentle sleep be yours forever
A soft hand rest your innocent heart so true
A wistful longing to hear once more
The warmth of laughter
The warmth of care
A wistful longing to feel once more
The innocence and purity of soul
A gentle soul of sweet innocence
Gone
Without a noise

Were we friends or were we sisters
As she called me once or twice

Light and love
For me she had
A childlike laugh
An open heart
A purity found rare
A sincerity beyond compare

So suddenly unexpected
A butterfly
Flitting here and there
So suddenly unexpected
Gone
Disappeared
Leaving behind fragile hearts
Crushed and pained

Understanding warmth
Strong and steady
Years of strength
Rock solid
Unraveling of the time glass hour

No time for jingle
No time for jangle
Just plain and simple

So true and pure
Just a soft chuckle in my ears

A steady understanding
A generosity of love
A care so genuine
So hard to forget

The humility
The humbleness
To accept and question not
The protective love freely given
For she recognized in me
The need for guiding care

Words of wisdom flowed from her
A surprising maturity
Which guided me
To see with clarity
The things surrounding me

Sleep in peace gentle one
Sleep in calm repose
Forever remembered
Never forgotten
In our hearts you still will be
~ Dee

116. Broken Flowers

Broken flowers in a jar
Mending them a job too far

Purple marks
And purple stains
Spot the petals
In the light

Celebrated on a moonlit night
Night is done
Day begun

Needed not anymore
And will be discarded
Near the door

Pray that we may never treat
Our own this way when needs we meet

- Dee

117. A Glance

Your eyes of laughter
Tell a tale
That only I will know
A glance made me come alive
It was too late then
When I learnt that it was love

~ Dee

118. Unkempt tenderness

Unkempt tenderness
Swept up in love
A child's chocolate flavored hug
They love
Because they do not know
How not to

~ Dee

119. 2020

When all of this is over and done
I will hug you close to me
Over a nice hot cup of tea

Where we will laugh
And talk of this and that
And a whole lot of other sense and nonsense

Until that day comes
Where we can sit and chat among the blooms
Hold me close in your mind and heart
And I'll hold you close in mine

~ Dee

120. The Charm

The sun rises with you
The sun sets with you
The moon cuddles you in her arms
The stars crown you with diamonds
The clouds caress your every care
The heavens move with your every breath
And when it rains
Therein lies your secret charm

~ Dee

121. A Gossamer Dream

A delicate creation
Words lack for expression
A wisp of fragility
A trace of lace
A delicate creation

I search imagination
For a name to name it
A silk
A gossamer bloom
More fine
Tenderly held
In the realms of the mind
A dulcet gossamer dream

~ Dee

122. The Rustle

Quiet corners of the mind gently stir
The Rustle
The Smell
The Touch
Of cream-colored pages
Keep company in solitude
While merging melting unnoticed
Into the chair

~ Dee

123. Drops of Light

Nights of fiery fire blossom in the velvet dark
Enchanting patterns of light and desire
Born and created in the charmed still air
Drops of Light
Drops of Brilliance
Luminous sprinkles of stars and sparks
Darkness
Adds beauty and magic to light
Complementing and completing the incomplete
Without darkness
There is no light
And without light
There is no dark

~ Dee

124. String of Words

There are some people
We turn to
Return to
Like the North Star
Wherever we are
The years gone by does not taint
Constancy in our hearts

Without speaking
Without meeting
For in our mind
Through distance and time
They were always there
Present in our hearts and minds

We remember their laughter
We remember their words
And when we meet again
We continue our string of words

~ Dee

125. Different Hearts

Grief comes out in different ways
Far be it for us to judge.

Sometimes sadness masquerades
As anger or fear in different space

Life by unfairness laced
Those who are left behind
Love them for who they are
Hug them for who they are

Limitless compassion
A softness reserved
For these gentle ones
With such heavy hearts
Caught in the cross winds of life

Forgive them for whatever they have said
Forgive them for whatever they have done
For different hearts
Handle sadness
In a million different ways

~ Dee

126. Just Being Me

The gentleness of a soft slow morning
Me and my tea in peace
Me and my soul alone
And reveling in just being me
Before the different roles start peering and appearing
With the responsibilities they bring of home and work
This time is just for me and my soul
And my tea
Meditation this is for me
~ Dee

127. Truthful Lies

The walls were down
The soul exposed
Vulnerability shone hard
The tears they came
Trickling down
None a perfect drop
Perfection was for instagrammed lives
And not for a basket of truthful lies

~ Dee

128. Until You Left

You never knew
How much you meant to me
And I never knew
Until you left

~ Dee

129. Walled Ice

And the wall of ice grew
And it hardened
And it deafened
Until love disappeared

~ Dee

130. Softspoken Smiles

The joy will never fade
Of a pure memory
Of sprinkled laughter
Of soft-spoken smiles
Of unspoken love
On rainy days

- Dee

131. Cloudy Days

I miss you
As the morning misses the sun
On a cloudy day
As the night misses the moon
On a starry night

~ Dee

132. Moonlit Aurora

Jasmine air tantalizes
Teases
Hangs in the air
At evenfall
The coolness of night
Slow descent
The moon softly fades in
Glancing a quizzical glance
Pensive
At feelings floating in air

With subtle touch
A hint of a smile
A slight nod of the head
Sweetness of innocence she pours
Stirred with love
Sprinkled with warmth
So delicate and precise
Yet
Undecipherable
Inexact
Whispered volumes in a single breath
Twilighted Dusk appears

Moon beams charmed by velvet sky
Lingering
For a glimpse of the sun
Dawn and it's time to go
But she can't bring herself to leave

The clouds burnished the sun
And he with brilliance awoke
A gentle illuminance he became
Radiating all aglow
To show the world
What he could become
Luminous in entirety

The moon whispered to him on a passing cloud
There are the stars, the sky, the clouds for me
And then there is you
And it is enough
All that you do
And you are enough
For me and for you
And then she softly fades away

~ Dee

133. Angels

Peals of laughter I do miss
Exceptional understanding of me
So careful and considerate
With a spirit so rare
Wish I could hug you one last time
And have just one last glance
So many wishes and wishes and wishes
When will it ever end

A closeness of heart
A kindred spirit of sort
Was unexpectedly bestowed on me
And I cherish my dear
I cherish it so
Every moment I saw you near

I miss you my dear
I miss you so
All those who held you dear
Miss you my dear
More than anyone else can know

You must be roaming in paradise
Happy and at peace
Glimpsing down from time to time
With a teasing smile
To see
This circus on earth
From hoop to hoop
To swinging from a trapeze
As we go about our life
Thinking it's routine

You are at peace
No more discomfort taint
Spirit of love with truth stained
No more pain

You are at peace
Your mind at rest
No more suffering
To bring unrest
~ Dee

134. Spaces

No matter how close the people
No matter how deep the love
We need spaces of quietness
Around us
Within us
Spaces of silence and peace

Spaces to think and ponder
Spaces to wonder about things
Worthy and unworthy
Not a matter
Spaces to just be

~ Dee

135. Unspoken Words

In lengthy words do not always lie
Sincerity serene
At times it is brevity ~ the shortest route
That can be trusted most
Sometimes it is silence most precious
Which speak unspoken words
Of love true and deep
In a warm held hand
A hug to keep
And a kiss to remember by
~ Dee

A Note Of Gratitude

To the wonderful people who inspired me to write.

To the wonderful people who took the time to read.

Thank you

www.ingramcontent.com/pod-product-compliance
Ingram Content Group UK Ltd.
Pitfield, Milton Keynes, MK11 3LW, UK
UKHW040006200726
13854UKWH00001B/62

9 798885 213677